MAHAMUDRA

His Holiness, the 16th Gyalwa Karmapa

MAHAMUDRA

BOUNDLESS JOY AND FREEDOM

A COMMENTARY ON THE WISHING PRAYER
FOR THE ATTAINMENT OF
THE ULTIMATE MAHAMUDRA
GIVEN BY HIS HOLINESS RANGJUNG DORJE
(THE THIRD KARMAPA, 1284–1339)

OLE NYDAHL

Blue Dolphin

For information, address: Blue Dolphin Publishing, Inc.
P.O. Box 1908 • Nevada City, CA 95959

Library of Congress Cataloging-in-Publication Data
Nydahl, Ole
    Mahamudra : boundless joy and freedom : a commentary on the
Tibetan Mahamudra text of the Third Karmapa, Rangjung Dorje,
1284–1339 / Ole Nydahl.
        p. cm.
    Includes English translation of the Mahamudra text.
    Includes bibliographical references.
    ISBN 0-931892-69-4 : $9.95
    1. Ran-byun-rdo-rje, Karma-pa III, 1284–1339. Nes don phyag rgya
chen po'i smon lam. 2. Kar-ma-pa (Sect)—Prayer-books and
devotions—Tibetan—History and criticism. 3. Mahamudra (Tantric
rite) I. Ran-byun-rdo-rje, Karma-pa III, 1284–1339. Nes don phyag
rgya chen po'i smon lam. English. 1991. II. Title.
BQ7682.6.N93 1991
294-3'44—dc20   91-26450
                                                                        CIP

Other books by Ole Nydahl
    *Entering the Diamond Way: My Path Among the Lamas
    Basic Dharma
    Practical Buddhism
    *Ngondro
    *Mahamudra
    Riding the Tiger: How the Buddhas Came to the West (forthcoming)
*These books are also available in Danish, German, and Spanish

Printed in the United States of America by
Blue Dolphin Press, Inc., Grass Valley, California

9   8   7   6   5   4   3   2   1

Table of Contents

Foreword

DEAREST FRIENDS EVERYWHERE: This small book is no eye-catcher among the several vast treatises on Mahamudra you can buy today. It contains, however, the transmission of my teachers, great meditation masters of the Karma Kagyu lineage, and will be usable in modern life situations. In a direct way, it is also a guide to the larger works.

This book is printed with much thanks due to the generosity of Tomek Lehnert and Roland Peters. Enjoy.

Yours,

Ole

Saraha

Introduction

MAHAMUDRA IS THE MOST EXCITING THING in the whole world: in the free fall, before the parachute opens, or in the midst of the most intense moments of love: who has the experience? Who has the joy, the excitement?

However you look, it is always our mind. One man may be poor and another rich, but the former feels that the world is his because the sky is wide and he has little to worry about. At the same time, the latter may doubt the meaning of his life because some unneeded money just slipped through his fingers.

Wherever we look and whatever we do, everything happens in our mind.

Mahamudra points directly to this mind: it is the state where the mind recognizes itself. Here it doesn't rely on its experiences. By resting in itself, awareness arises of its timeless essence. This unique text describes the experience. It is given by the master of yogis, the Third Karmapa (Rangjung Dorje) in the form of a wishing prayer.

A common reaction when first contacting the Mahamudra is a gut feeling of trust and the intellectual joy that something like this can exist. Then one grows with the view and, gradually or quickly, depending on the impressions in our mind, liberation and enlightenment become things one can relate to.

Twenty-five hundred years ago, the Buddha taught three types of people. First, there were those who wanted to get rid of their own difficulties. Second were ones who were interested in a rich inner life, in philosophy and psychology, and who wanted to do something for others; and finally, the people who directly trusted the perfect nature of mind. The teachings for each of these groups consisted of three steps: how cause and effect function on the level of one's practice; meditation, to clear the way from concepts to experience; and finally, how to receive the achieved insight, how not to lose it again.

Mahamudra was given for the third kind of people, as were the formal transmissions we know as initiations. Directly or indirectly, seeds of enlightenment are planted in our mind.

With time, they transform all experience into a pure realm. While the formal initiations are given in ritual situations, here are some examples of the direct way:

Once, 1100 years ago, Tilopa and Naropa were walking along a road in northern India. Naropa, a former professor, saw everything colored by his many concepts—when suddenly a snake was lying there, looking just as complicated as his mind. Tilopa touched the snake with a stick, and as they watched it sliding off, he asked: "What happens to your thoughts when they disappear, Naropa, how real are they then?"

There are countless examples of such transmissions in the Kagyu lineage: Once Rechungpa was sitting in front of Milarepa, totally unhappy about what he considered his lack of progress. As he was expressing this, Milarepa joked with him and at the same time transferred a very strong blessing directly to his heart center. Rechungpa was "blown away" and in a moment made a huge leap towards enlightenment. This method, where the teacher shares his power directly with the student, brings immediate results. Here, awakening happens without symbol or concept, simply by the sharing of space and awareness.

Different cultures and situations give access to such states in unintended ways. For instance in Europe, we may travel along the Autobahn at 140 MPH, enjoying the excitement and freedom of superb motoring for hours. This exhilaration thoroughly removes boundaries. Gradually it becomes less necessary to talk, because all say the same anyway. A similar sharing, but of the conscious enlightened qualities of space, is the gift of the Third Karmapa, Rangjung Dorje, to us here. Through the skillful means of a "wishing prayer," he enables us to hook onto his experience and gradually make it our own.

The Mahamudra that the Buddha gave to his closest students, came to Tibet twice. The first time it was introduced by the great Guru Rinpoche around 750 A.D. When he left Tibet, one of his main consorts, Yeshe Tsogyal, held the rudder till a king called Langdarma turned against the Buddhists. Most of this first transmission was destroyed, leaving the so-called Termas, the teachings he had hidden to inspire later times.

About 1000 A.D., the Mahamudra came to Tibet again, with the teacher Marpa. The first time it was called Dzog Chen or Maha-Ati; now the name was Chag Chen or Mahamudra. Three hundred years later only one man held the teachings of Dzog Chen, otherwise they would have disappeared—the third Karmapa, Rangjung Dorje. At the same time, through Milarepa, Gampopa and the earlier Karmapas, he was the natural heir to the Mahamudra as well. As the text shows, he was also well versed in an important school of philosophy, the Uma Chenpo or Madhyamika. Its two aspects, Rang-tong and Shen-tong, correspond to a neutral or intellectual, and a positive or experiential view of "emptiness," or conditioned nature of all things. These are the Sutra level of teachings.

Many give marvelous explanations on the Mahamudra. If you ask them how it feels, however, they have little to say. Their intellectual studies didn't tell them that. Actually, it is the most powerful and total of experiences. It is not being able to rationalize a lot of things, but the most intense joy, courage and love—like holding our fingers in the main socket and pulling the town's electricity through our bones.

Today some may see it as plagiarism that the Karmapa brings together the best from all lineages, but here it is not a question of stealing quotes. The intensity of full enlightenment is the primary thing, beyond all concepts, and here it is made accessible to us in the terminologies of three of the four main Tibetan schools.

For the last 700 years, all the Buddha's teachings on the absolute nature of mind have thus existed in our Mahamudra transmission. Around 1980, in our retreat center at Rodby, near the ferry to Germany in Southern Denmark, V. Ven. Tenga Rinpoche spent three weeks going through this text. He is the meditation master to whom H.H. the Karmapa entrusted the education of his lineage. Hannah translated it into Danish and I into German. Frequently since then, and around the world, I have gone through the text in week-long courses or skimmed its main content in one evening in a super-short form. There is no doubt that our Western maturity, motivation and level of knowledge make it possible to extract the main content in this way. Starting with the Karmapa's blessing, maintaining a complete trust in the nature of mind, and adding to this the wish to be of use to all beings, those with the right karmic seeds will have benefit from working with this text.

For the full realization of Mahamudra, however, there are two classical ways to approach the lineage. Both go through the main Indian teachers of Marpa, who gave him their full transmissions. One is the well-known Naropa, and the other the lesser mentioned Maitripa. In Tibet the way of the former was most frequently used, but in the West where we must also earn money and can rarely do long retreats or lead extreme ways of life, the latter may become more popular. Both ways are actually contained in our Karmapa practice, the most direct of all.

As always, we start by examining our situation. Here we discover four important things: That this life offers the precious conditions for practicing and becoming enlightened for the benefit of all. That we should use the chance now. We don't know how long we will live, and only the mind will always remain. That cause and effect function. That everything we do, think and say will become our future. And finally, why to meditate: Enlightenment is highest, unceasing joy, and we can do little for others while confused ourselves.

Seeing one's present inability to decide how to feel, it is natural to look for someone who can teach us. Here we find the Buddha—not as a man, god, or historical figure, but as an example and a living energy. We see him as a mirror of our own enlightened qualities and take refuge in him. Next we open ourselves to his teachings which bring us to that state called Dharma, and to our friends and helpers on the way, the Sangha, the Practicing Ones. For quickest results, we especially take refuge in the Lama. He gives us the abundant warmth to melt away all doubts and tightness, the methods to fully open our potential, and we receive the help of Black

Coat and the other lineage-protectors who make strong and
quick development possible. In the Karma Kagyu lineage the
Lama is always the Karmapa, and all other lamas are working
in his name.

After refuge follows Ngöndro, the Preparatory Practices.
I know that a lama in America started his students meditating
without this foundation, but I hardly know anybody praising
their development. All the meditation masters of our lineage,
headed by H.H. the Karmapa, call these preliminaries the
basis of the Diamond Way. Enlightenment is reached after a
long journey and whoever starts with only a gallon of gas will
be left somewhere along the road.

The practices accumulate both good impressions and
wisdom. First one purifies mainly the body through prostra-
tions, and mind and speech by doing the hundred-syllable
Purification mantras, then one fills the resultant mental space
with great richness through the Mandala offerings, and finally
one receives the blessing of the lineage through meditating
on the Lama, the so-called Guru-Yoga.

Ngöndro is at the beginning of both Naropa's and Maitripa's ways, but then they separate. The former goes on with
a series of "means," seeing oneself externally, internally, and

then on a secret level as a form of energy and light. Here a red, transparent and dancing female Buddha is often chosen.

The next stage consists of the "Six Doctrines." They start up our system of inner energies. Through concentrations, deep breathing and the blessing of the lineage, some things happen to make us wish our school-money back.

When a team of scientists from Stanford University visited the H.H. the Dalai Lama early in 1988 to look into the typical effects of Tibetan meditation, he sent them straight to the Karmapa's main center, Rumtek in Sikkim, where V.Ven. Bokar Tulku and some other yogis found time for them. The results must be already out in their publications, and I can tell you that it took a long time before they trusted their electrodes and other instruments. Talking with Bokar Tulku in Bodh Gaya, north-west India, a few days after, he said with an angelic smile, "I simply prayed to the Karmapa, that's all."

The "Third Initiation" on Naropa's way works with sexual energies, our greatest power. Here, through control of the former steps of meditation, with a spiritual partner—or extra-good imagination for celibates—very quick enlighten-

ment is possible. Here, unceasing space-joy-awareness naturally blends into the Mahamudra. This is the "Way of Means."

After Ngöndro, Maitripa's way starts with Zhi-nay, a
method to hold and strengthen the mind. From this arises a
state of intense inspiration and clear insight, called Lhag-tong
or Vipassana. This leads into the experience of subject, object
and action as interdependent and one. The way of insight can
be practiced with or without a meditation-form "Yidam." To
Hannah and me, H.H. the Karmapa said that the complete
practice of meditating on the Lama, "Guru-Yoga," combines
and goes beyond both.

Concerning the steps of access into this Mahamudra
state, I will quote Kunzig Shamarpa in Germany in 1990. He
said that there is a special Mahamudra which is H.H. the
Karmapa's essence but which the world was too crazy to allow
the 16th Karmapa to pass on. For that we shall have to wait
till his 17th incarnation. It permits us to transform into
rainbows in about a week.

Then there are the ways called Chag-Chen and Dzog-
Chen, permitting full enlightenment in this life; and a slower,
sutra-and-philosophy-based way taught in the Gelugpa tra-
dition. The medium way fits most students of the Karmapa

today. It consists of four steps into Mahamudra. The first one is one-pointedness, meaning that we change our mind with so many good impressions that it will stay contentedly wherever it is. This is actually a pleasure. Not having to run from or after anything frees great joy in our mind.

Non-artificiality comes next. There is now no need to play games anymore, and one becomes natural. The third step is that everything gets the taste of freshness and actuality of here and now. The radiance of awareness itself becomes much more powerful than the varying objects and states manifesting in it.

Finally we reach the level that is beyond all striving, called non-meditation. Here everything fits just as it is and because it is. It doesn't mean that from then on we just take it easy, but instead that from a state of "resting in what is," all perfect qualities of body, speech and mind will manifest freely, and for the benefit of all.

This, then, is the frame I think a Westerner needs. Now follows the Mahamudra text of the Third Karmapa, Rangjung Dorje, a wishing prayer given about 700 years ago. We will first look at the verses in Hannah's translation and then I will add what seems meaningful to us today.

The Third Karmapa, Rangjung Dorje (1284–1339)

ༀ། །དེས་དོན་ཕྱག་རྒྱ་ཆེན་པོའི་སྨོན་ལམ་

ཞེས་བྱ་བ་རྗེ་རང་བྱུང་རྡོ་རྗེས་མཛད་པའོ། །

Wishing prayer for the attainment of
the ultimate Mahamudra.
Given by His Holiness Rangjung Dorje
(The Third Karmapa)

༉ །རོ་མོ་གུ་ད།

སྒྲ་མ་རྣམས་དང་ཨེ་དམ་འཁྲིད་འོར་ར་ལྔ།།

ཐྱོགས་བཅུ་དུས་གསུམ་རྒྱལ་བ་སྲས་དང་བཅས།།

བདག་ལ་བརྩེར་དགོངས་བདག་གི་སྨོན་ལམ་རྣམས།།

ཇི་བཞིན་འགྲུབ་པའི་མཐུན་འགྱུར་བྱིན་རླབས་མཛོད།།

༈ །བདག་དང་མཁའ་ཡམ་སེམས་ཅན་ཐམས་ཅད་ཀྱི།།

བསམ་སྦྱོར་རྣམ་དག་གདངས་རེ་ལམ་སྐྱེས་བའི།།

འཁོར་གསུམ་རྟོག་མེད་དགེ་ཚོགས་ཆུ་རྒྱུན་རྣམས།།

རྒྱལ་བ་སྐུ་བཞིའི་ཆུ་མཚོར་འདུག་གྱུར་ཅིག།

You Lamas, Yidams and Protectors of the power
    circles,
You victorious Buddhas and your Bodhisattva
    sons of the ten directions and the three times,
Think lovingly of us and give your blessings
That our wishes may be fulfilled exactly as they
    are made.

Arising from the snow mountain of the perfectly
    pure thoughts and actions of ourselves and all
    beings,
May the river of good deeds, unsullied by the
    concept of a separation into three,
Flow into the ocean of the four Buddha-states.

༄༅། །རྗེ་སྤྲིན་དེ་མ་ཚབ་པ་འི་སྤྲིན་དུ།།

སྐྱེ་དང་སྐྱེ་བཚེ་རབས་ཀུན་ཏུ་ཡང་།།

སྤྱིག་དང་སྤྱག་བ་སྤྱལ་སྐྱུ་ཡདམི་སྐྲག་ཅིད།།

བདེ་དགེ་རྒྱུ་མཚོའི་དཔལ་ལ་སྤྱོད་པར་ཤོག།

༄༅། །དཔལ་འཁྲུར་མཚོག་ཚབ་དད་བཙུན་འཇེས་རབ་ཁུན།།

ངའེས་གཉེན་བཟང་བསྟེན་གདམས་པའི་བཅུད་ཚབ་ནས།།

ཚོལ་བཞིན་བསྒྲུབ་ལ་རར་ཆད་མ་མཆིས་པར།།

ཚེ་རབས་ཀུན་ཏུ་དམ་ཆོས་སྤྱོད་པར་ཤོག།

Until that happens, may we, in all lifetimes, from
    one birth to the next,
Never once hear the sound of pain or suffering,
But instead experience oceans of radiant goodness
    and joy.

Having attained a free and fully endowed birth,
A precious human life with confidence, diligence,
    and wisdom,
Relying upon a spiritual teacher and receiving his
    Essential instructions,
May we then practice the precious teachings
    without hindrance in this and all future lives.

༄༅། །ཕྱུང་རིགས་ཆོས་པས་མི་ཤེས་སྒྲིབ་ལས་གྲོལ།།

མན་ངག་བརྨ་པས་རེ་ཚ་མ་སྱུན་ནག་བཙམ།།

སྒོམ་རྒྱང་འོད་ཀྱིས་གནས་ལུགས་རེ་བཞིན་གསལ།།

འཞེས་རྡབ་གསུམ་སྐྱེ་སྱུང་བ་རྒྱས་པར་འོག།

༄༅། །རྟོག་ཆད་མཐའ་བྲལ་བདེན་གཉིས་གཞི་ཡི་དོན།།

སྒྲོ་སྐུར་མཐའ་བྲལ་ཚོགས་གཉིས་ལམ་མཆོག་གིས།།

སྲིད་ཞིའི་མཐའ་བྲལ་དོན་གཉིས་འབྲས་ཐོབ་པའི།།

གོལ་འཆུག་མེད་པའི་ཆོས་དང་ཕྱུད་པར་འོག།

Hearing the teachings frees us from the veils
of ignorance.
Contemplating the Oral instructions removes the
darkness of doubt.
The light arising from meditation makes clear the
nature of mind, exactly as it is.
May the light of these three wisdoms increase.

May we receive the flawless teachings, the
foundation of which are the two truths which
are free from the extremes of eternalism and
nihilism,
And through the supreme path of the two
accumulations, free from the extremes of
negation and affirmation,
May we obtain the fruit which is free from the
extremes of either,
Dwelling in the conditioned state or in the state of
only peace.

༄༅། །སྐྱུང་གཞི་སེམས་ཉིད་གསལ་སྟོང་ཟུང་འཇུག་ལ། །

སྟོང་ཉིད་ཕྱག །ཆེན་རྡོ་རྗེའི་རྣལ་འབྱོར་ཆེས། །

བྱུང་ཚུ་རྒྱུ་ཐུར་ལ་བྲུལ་བའི་རྡི་མ་རྣམས། །

སྤྱངས་འབྱང་རྡི་བྲུལ་ཆོས་སྐུ་མངོན་གྱུར་ཡོད། །

༄༅། །གཞི་ལ་སྒྱུ་འཛིགས་ཆོད་པ་ལྷུ་བའི་གདེངས། །

དེ་ལ་མ་ཡེངས་སྟོང་བ་སྒོམ་པའི་གནད། །

སྒོམ་དོན་ཀུན་ལ་ཙལ་སྟོང་སྒྱིང་བའི་མཚོག །

ལྷུ་སྒོམ་སྒྱིད་པའི་གདེངས་དང་ལྡན་པར་ཡོད

The basis of purification is the mind itself in its
 union of clarity and emptiness.
The method of purification is the great
 Mahamudra Diamond-practice.
What is to be purified are the transitory illusory
 impurities.
The fruit of the purification is the perfectly pure
 truth-state.
May this become realized.

Overcoming doubts concerning the fundamental
 teaching gives trust in the view.
Protecting this view without distraction is the
 essence of meditation.
Correct meditation in itself is best behavior.
May we trust the view, the meditation and the
 conduct.

༈ །ཆོས་རྣམས་ཐམས་ཅད་སེམས་ཀྱི་རྣམ་འཕྲུལ་ཏེ།།

སེམས་ནི་སེམས་མེད་སེམས་ཀྱི་ངོ་བོས་སྟོང་།།

སྐྱེ་ཞིང་མ་འགགས་ཅིར་ཡང་སྣང་བ་སྟེ།།

ལེགས་པར་བརྟགས་ནས་གཞི་རྩ་ཆོད་པར་ཤོག།

༈ །ཡོད་མ་མྱོང་བའི་རང་སྣང་ཕྱལ་དུ་འབྱོལ།

མ་རིག་དབང་གིས་རང་རིག་བདག་ཏུ་འཁྲུལ།

གཉིས་འཛིན་དབང་གིས་སྲིད་པའི་ཀློང་དུ་འཁྱམས།

མ་རིག་འཁྲུལ་པའི་རྩད་དར་ཆོད་པར་ཤོག

All phenomena are projections of the mind.
Mind is not "a" mind; the mind is empty
   in essence.
Although empty, everything constantly arises in it.
Through the deepest examination of the mind
   may we find its innermost root.

Self-manifestation, which has never existed as
   such, is erroneously seen as an object.
Through ignorance, self-awareness is mistakenly
   experienced as an "I."
Through attachment to this duality we are caught
   in the conditioned world.
May the root of confusion be found.

༄༅། །ཡོད་པ་མ་ཡིན་རྒྱལ་བས་ཀྱང་མ་གཟིགས།།

མེད་པ་མ་ཡིན་འཁོར་འདས་ཀུན་གྱི་གཞི།།

འགལ་འདུན་མ་ཡིན་ཟུང་འཇུག་དབུ་མའི་ལམ།།

མཐའ་བྲལ་སེམས་ཀྱི་ཆོས་ཉིད་རྟོགས་པར་ཤོག།

༄༅། །འདི་ཡིན་ཞེས་པ་གང་གིས་མཚོན་པ་མེད།།

འདི་མིན་ཞེས་བྱ་གང་གིས་བཀག་པ་མེད།།

རྟོ་ལས་འདས་པའི་ཆོས་ཉིད་འདུས་མ་བྱས།།

ཡང་དག་དོན་གྱི་མཐའ་ནི་དེར་པར་ཤོག།

It is not existent—for even the Buddhas do not
    see it.
It is not non-existent, being the basis for both
    samsara and nirvana.
It is not the opposites, nor both, nor something
    else, but rather their union—the middle way.
May we realize the true nature of mind, which is
    beyond extremes.

It cannot be described by saying, "It is."
It cannot be denied by saying, "It is not."
The incomprehensible absolute reality is not
    composite.
May we achieve certainty about the correctness of
    this ultimate meaning.

༄༅། །འདི་ཉིད་མ་རྟོགས་འཁོར་བའི་རྒྱུ་མཚན་ད་འཁིར་ད།།

འདི་ཉིད་རྟོགས་ན་ཁབ་པ་རྒྱས་གཞན་ན་མེད།།

ཐམས་ཅད་འདི་ཡིན་འདི་མིན་གང་ཡང་མེད།།

ཚས་ཉིད་ཀུན་གཞིའི་མཚང་ནི་རིག་པར་འོག།

༄༅། །སྣང་ཡང་སེམས་ལ་སྟོང་ཡང་སེམས་ཡིན་ཏེ།།

རྟོགས་ཀྱང་སེམས་ལ་འཁྲུལ་ཡང་རང་གི་སེམས།།

སྐྱེ་ར་ཀྱང་སེམས་ལ་འགགས་ཀྱང་སེམས་ཡིན་ས།།

བློ་འདོགས་ཐམས་ཅད་སེམས་ལ་ཚོད་པར་འོག།།

As long as this is not recognized, the wheel of
    existence turns.
When this is understood, the state of Buddha is
    nothing other than that.
There is nothing that can be described as either
    existing or not existing.
May the nature of reality, the true nature of the
    Buddha mind, be recognized.

Appearance is only mind, emptiness is only mind,
    enlightenment is only mind, and confusion is
    only one's own mind.
Arising is only mind; disappearance is only mind.
May every doubt and hesitation that concerns the
    mind be overcome.

ༀ། །ཁྲིམ་ཅུས་ཚུལ་བའི་སྐྲམ་ཁྲིམ་མ་བསྒྲུད་ཅིང་།།

ཐ་མལ་འདུ་འཛིའི་རྫུང་གིས་མ་བསྐྱུང་པར།།

མ་བཅོར་གཏུག་ག་མ་རང་རབ་འཛིག་ཞེས་པའི།།

སེམས་ཉིད་ཉམས་ལེན་སྐྱངས་ཤིང་སྐྱོང་བར་ཤོག །

ༀ། །ཕྱ་རྐགས་རྟག་པའི་དཔའ་རྣབས་རང་སར་ཞི།།

གཡོ་མེད་སེམས་ཀྱི་ཅུ་བོ་དང་གིས་གནས།།

ཁྱིང་རྒྱགས་རྙོག་པའི་དྲི་མ་དང་བྲལ་བའི།།

ཞི་གནས་རྒྱ་མཚོ་མི་གཡོ་བརྟན་པར་ཤོག །

May we neither be sullied by forced intellectual
meditation nor disturbed by the winds of
everyday life.
May we skillfully hold onto our practice
concerning the nature of mind.

May the immovable ocean of meditative peace,
Where the waves of subtle and gross thoughts
come to rest through their own power, and
Where the waters of the unmoving mind remain
in themselves,
Unspotted by laziness, sleepiness or unclarity,
become stable.

༄༅། །བསྒྱུར་མདེ་སེམས་ལ་ཡང་ཡང་བལྟས་པའི་ཚེ།།

མཐོང་མེད་དོན་ནི་ཇེ་བཞིན་ལྷུག་གིར་མཐོང་།།

ཡིན་མིན་དོན་ལ་ཏྲེ་ཚོམ་ཆོད་པ་ཉིད།།

འཁྲུལ་མེད་རང་ཁོ་རང་གིས་ཤེས་པར་ཤོག།

༄༅། །ཕྱལ་ལ་བལྟས་པས་ཕྱལ་མེད་སེམས་སུ་མཐོང་།།

སེམས་ལ་དབྱུས་པས་སེམས་མེད་དཔོས་སྟོང་།།

གཉིས་ལ་བལྟས་པས་གཉིས་འཛིན་རང་སར་གྲོལ།།

ཉིད་གསལ་སེམས་ཀྱི་གནས་ལུགས་རྟོགས་པར་ཤོག།

If again and again we examine the mind, which
    cannot be examined,
We see that which cannot be seen, with total
    clarity, just as it is.
May the faultless mind, freed from all doubts
    about being and not being, recognize itself.

Through the examination of external objects we
    see the mind, not the objects.
Through the examination of the mind we see its
    empty essence, but not the mind.
Through the examination of both, attachment to
    duality disappears by itself.
May the clear light, the true essence of mind, be
    recognized.

ༀ། །ཡིད་བྱེད་བྲལ་བ་འདི་ནི་ཕྱག་རྒྱ་ཆེ།།

མཐར་དང་བྲལ་བ་དབུ་མ་ཆེན་པོ་ཡིན།།

འདི་ནི་ཀུན་འདུས་རྫོགས་ཆེན་ཞེས་ཀྱང་ཟྲ།།

གཅིག་ཤེས་ཀུན་དོན་རྟོགས་པའི་གདེངས་ཐོང་ཕོག།

ༀ། །ཞེན་པ་མེད་པའི་རདེ་ཆེན་རྒྱུན་ཆད་མེད།།

མཆན་འཛིན་མེད་པའི་འོད་གསལ་སྒྲིབ་གཡོགས་བྲལ།།

བློ་ལས་འདས་པའི་མི་རྟོག་ལྷུན་གྱིས་གྲུབ།།

རྩོལ་མེད་ངང་ས་སྐྱོང་རྒྱུན་ཆད་མེད་པར་ཕོག།

Being without intellectual concepts, it is called the
Great Sign, or Mahamudra.
Being without extremes, it is called the Great
Middle Way, or Madhyamika.
As it embraces everything, it is called the Great
Perfection, or Maha-Ati.
May we have the confidence that the experience of
one is the experience of the meaning of all.

May we constantly and effortlessly experience the
never-ending highest joy, which is without
attachment,
The clear light that is without categories or veils
of obscuration, and
The spontaneous, concept-free state that is beyond
intellect.

༉། །བཟང་ཞིན་དམས་ཀྱི་འཛིན་པ་རང་སར་གྲོལ།།

ཐ་ཚིག་འཁྲུལ་པ་རང་བཞིན་འཆྱིངས་སུ་དག།

ཐ་མལ་ཤེས་པ་སྐྱད་བྱུང་རྒྱལ་ཚབ་མེད།།

སྟོས་ཐུལ་ཆོས་ཉིད་བདེན་པ་རྟོགས་པར་འོག།

༉། །འགྲོ་བའི་རང་བཞིན་རྟག་ཏུ་སངས་རྒྱས་ཀྱང་།།

མ་རྟོག་དབང་གིས་མཐའ་མེད་འཁོར་བར་འཁྱམས།།

དྲག་བསྒྱལ་མུ་མཐའ་མེད་པའི་སེམས་ཅན་ལ།།

བཟོད་མེད་སྙིང་རྗེ་རྒྱུད་ལ་སྐྱེ་བར་འོག།

Attachment to pleasant experiences vanishes of its
    own accord.
Illusory and negative thoughts are in their essence
    pure, like space.
In that simple state of mind there is nothing that
    must be given up or developed, avoided or
    attained.
May the truth of the uncomplicated nature of
    reality be realized.

Although the true nature of beings is always the
    Buddha essence,
Still we always wander in the ceaseless wheel of
    life, not understanding that.
May infinite compassion arise for the limitless
    suffering of all beings.

ༀ། །བཅོད་མེད་སྙིང་རྗེའི་རྩལ་པང་མ་འགགས་པའི།།

བརྗེ་དུམ་དོ་བོ་སྤྱོང་དོན་རྟེན་པར་འར།།

རྱང་འཇུག་གོལ་ས་སྒྲལ་པའི་ལམ་མཆོག་འདི།།

འཕྲལ་མེད་ཉིན་མཚན་ཀུན་ཏུ་བསྒོམ་པར་ཤོག།།

ༀ། །སྒོམ་རྒྱབས་ལས་རྱང་སྤྱན་དང་མངོན་ཤེས་དང་།།

སེམས་ཅན་སྤྲིན་བྱམ་སངས་རྒྱམ་ཞིང་རབ་སྦྱངམ།།

སངས་རྒྱས་ཆོས་རྣམས་འགྲུབ་པའི་སྨོན་ལམ་རྫོགས།།

རྫོགས་སྨིན་སྦྱངས་གསུམ་ལཧར་ཕྱིན་སངས་རྒྱས་ཤོག།།

Although this infinite compassion is strong and
    unceasing,
The truth of its empty nature arises nakedly the
    very moment it appears.
This union of emptiness and compassion is the
    highest faultless way.
May we meditate inseparable from it, the whole
    time, day and night.

May we attain the state of Buddha through
    maturity, realization, and completion,
And develop beings through "divine eyes" and
    "clear sight" arising through the power of
    meditation.
May we realize the Buddha fields and fulfill the
    wishing prayer of the perfection of the
    Buddha qualities.

༄༅། །ཕྱག་མ་བཅུའི་རྒྱལ་བ་སྐུ་མ་བཅས་ཐུགས་རྗེ་དང་། །

རྣམ་དཀར་དགེ་བ་རྗེ་སྐྱེད་ཡོད་པའི་མཐུས།།

དེ་ལྟར་བདག་དང་སེམས་ཅན་ཁམས་ཅད་ཀྱི།།

སྨོན་ལམ་རྣམ་དག་རྗེ་བཞིན་འགྲུབ་གྱུར་ཅིག།

You Buddhas and Bodhisattvas from the ten direc-
    tions,
Through your compassion and through the power
    of all the pure and good that exists,
May the pure wishing prayers of ourselves and all
    beings be fulfilled,
Just as they were made.

Milarepa, surrounded by Kagyu lineage

Commentary

THE TEXT BEGINS BY GIVING HOMAGE:

You Lamas, Yidams and Protectors of the power
    circles,
You victorious Buddhas and your Bodhisattva
    sons of the ten directions and the three times,
Think lovingly of us and give your blessings
That our wishes may be fulfilled exactly as they
    are made.

IF SOMETHING IS TO GROW, first there must be a field. Then we
need seeds, sun and rain. These together make it happen.
So also is our way to enlightenment, but as this is a diamond-
way practice, we don't involve the "outer" Refuge of the Three
Jewels, the Buddha, his Teachings and the Practicing Ones,
but rather our Lama, the Yidams and Protectors of our lineage.
They are the inner refuge or "three roots" which bring about
our development. The power circles are the palaces of energy

and fulfillment which constantly surround enlightened beings. They condense out of space from their thirty-seven perfect qualities and are shared also by other Buddhas with similar activity. The energy-circles are surrounded by powerful protectors and we should know that these are always there, even when not depicted on Thangkas or included in the meditation texts.

Why do we call the Buddhas Victorious? Because they have removed all disturbing feelings. Even if we kill masses of enemies, they will only become more numerous. Negative energies will always get stuck on our hooks of aggression which project into the world. If we conquer all anger inside ourselves, however, there is no point of contact for negativity, and angry people have to go elsewhere to fight.

Bodhisattva sons: Today we can joyfully drop the gender. Many speculate about the differences between Buddhas and Bodhisattvas and in practice one can see it like this: Bodhisattvas can do many things and Buddhas all things.

That our wishes may be fulfilled exactly as they are made: The final wish is a bit strange to Westerners who have total trust once they open up. It sounds as if the Buddhas might pull a joke on us at the very end.

THE NEXT VERSE TOUCHES A POETIC VIEW.

Arising from the snow mountain of the perfectly
pure thoughts and actions of ourselves and all
beings,
May the river of good deeds, unsullied by the
concept of a separation into three,
Flow into the ocean of the four Buddha-states.

THE GENERAL PICTURE IS CLEAR, but the Karmapa uses a term that is unusually severe, that of "unsullied." If someone whose mind is so strong declares something to be negative, the effect is enormous. Whoever is strong must also be kind.

Why, then, the choice of this word? The impurity implied is the fundamental one causing all suffering, at all times and places. It is the experience of separation between the seer, the thing seen and the act of seeing, between subject, object and action. Basic ignorance essentially means experiencing space as separation, not as a container holding us and all things. Looking through the glasses of either/or instead of both/and, we are either poor, causing attachment, or vulnerable, bringing about aversion and anger.

Attachment then condenses into greed, anger into hatred, and envy and stupidity produce pride. These bring about mixed thoughts, words and actions which are again followed by unpleasant results, causing us to find faults elsewhere and plant seeds of more suffering. Losing our feeling of totality, then, is no small impurity.

The four Buddha states are: Space as information, as all-knowingness, highest wisdom, and Potential. This is the Truth-state or Dharmakaya. The rich play of space, its constant freshness, is the state of joy or Sambhogakaya, and its spontaneous compassionate activity is the state of love or Nirmanakaya. One may compare the truth-state with water vapor in the atmosphere; it is there, but cannot be seen. The joy state is like clouds that come and go, and the compassionate state is the rain, which enables things to grow. A fourth "essential" state called Svabhavikakaya expresses that each of the preceding states is water, H_2O, and partakes of the same essence. Timeless awareness of this is the Buddha state.

THE NEXT VERSE MAKES WISHES FOR OUR WAY.

Until that happens, may we, in all lifetimes, from
    one birth to the next,
Never once hear the sound of pain or suffering,
But instead experience oceans of radiant goodness
    and joy.

UNTIL ENLIGHTENMENT WE ALL WANT TO REACH A KARMIC LEVEL
from where there is only upward progression, a Pure
Land. Then follows some Buddhist motivation-building,
showing us what we are able to do.

Having attained a free and fully endowed birth,
A precious human life with confidence, diligence
    and wisdom,
Relying upon a spiritual teacher and receiving his
    Essential instructions,
May we then practice the precious teachings
    without hindrance in this and all future lives.

FOR A LIFE TO BE FULLY ENDOWED and lead us towards enlightenment, several conditions must meet. There are eight hindrances which must be avoided, five factors we need from others, and another five must arise from our own situation. (See Nydahl, *Ngöndro,* 1990). The human birth we have is valuable because of confidence, diligence and wisdom. Confidence doesn't mean belief. One can doubt one's whole way to enlightenment if one is constructive enough to add one solved question to the last one and not always doubt the same thing. This is not the quick way, however. If one can incorporate other peoples' experiences, there is immense power there.

Diligence is always important. With it one doesn't only grow older, as all do, but life takes on extra dimensions. Our energy level is one of the tendencies most directly transferred from one life to the next and we decide here and now how much punch we wish to have for future times. The wisdom necessary here is very much the discriminating one—without that we waste our time. If we do spiritual shopping, running from one Lama to another and not forgetting to include the great swami Suchabanana, everything may feel sublime and spiritual, but neither terminology nor transmissions fit, and in the end we have heads the size of watermelons and hearts like hazelnuts. The maturity that shows us what is what and that keeps us with one thing—that is, we have real experience and are not just comparing words—is truly indispensible. If no inner sirens of warning start howling in us when something spiritually mixed, sentimental or shallow is served up in new-age sauce, real development is not possible.

The Buddhist privilege, above all, is being able to get teachings that point directly to the mind. What is good and bad—we say useful or harmful—everybody is told from childhood, but who will show us convincingly that our true essence is clear and limitless space, opening up our full potential for joy, compassion and trust? Only a true yogi, somebody carrying that conviction in his bones, can do that, and it is not enough that he convinces us through his personal example, he must also show ways we can use to get there.

THE FIFTH VERSE ALSO CONTAINS GENERAL BUDDHIST KNOWLEDGE.

Hearing the teachings frees us from the veils
   of ignorance.
Contemplating the Oral instructions removes the
   darkness of doubt.
The light arising from meditation makes clear the
   nature of mind, exactly as it is.
May the light of these three wisdoms increase.

THE KARMAPA HERE SHOWS THE THREE REQUIREMENTS for our practice: Obtaining correct information, having the chance to clarify questions and doubts, and receiving methods—meditations—which transform understanding into experience and growth. Meeting with all three may sound easy but is in fact very difficult. Nearly all Asians restrict themselves to the first. They go to the Buddha for economical or moral upliftment. Attending beautiful ceremonies, sponsoring initiations or taking blessings, they expect a long life, more money or more sons, but they don't want to ask questions. If there is a teaching, they also don't come. Perhaps something said might compel them to change their way of thinking and they don't want that. They consume Buddhism and prefer to believe that one must wear robes in order to meditate. Giving their offerings, they expect the monks to do the rest.

We in the West go to the other extreme. We only want to meditate. We are idealistic, romantic and want to experience things. Having studied for twenty years, when we step away from what we consider rationality, we want to feel things in a total way. What concerns inner development we want to trust, not discriminate and check. If the experiences are unusual and strong enough, we are certain that is real growth.

The third group opting for only one of the three requirements are the people who just want to discuss. They neither take the time to get real information, nor do they check it in meditation, and as voices get louder, or arguments slicker, the real losers are clarity and logic.

Only all conditions together bring about that clear light of certitude and insight which is our goal.

THE NEXT VERSE IS VERY CONCENTRATED. It contains the material for a full Buddhist lecture. As you will see, the key words are "without extremes."

May we receive the flawless teachings, the
    foundation of which are the two truths which
    are free from the extremes of eternalism and
    nihilism,
And through the supreme Path of the two
    accumulations, free from the extremes of
    negation and affirmation,
May we obtain the fruit which is free from the
    extremes of either,
Dwelling in the conditioned state or in the state of
    only peace.

WE WILL UNRAVEL IT FROM THE BEGINNING. Why are the teachings flawless?—because they bring results. They lead us to the goals of liberation and enlightenment, taking us first beyond suffering and then bestowing unlimited power to benefit all beings.

The two truths are the absolute truth of the emptiness, clarity and limitlessness of the mind, and the relative truth of how one gets there.

Knowing only about the goal, but having no way there, one is a dry intellectual. Knowing only the relative truth, but not where it should lead, one is in an unknown country without a map. Often the two truths are compared to eyes and legs. We only benefit when both are together.

Eternalism and nihilism? Eternalism covers the areas of both materialism and the much-praised realism. Whichever name one uses, the view is still limited. If things truly exist, also illness, old age and death are real. So is ultimate suffering and loss.

The other extreme, nihilism, also doesn't hold, and in two ways. On the inner level all things lose their fun and freshness, and on the outer nothing functions if we don't honor cause and effect. Nihilism crops up as a fad from time to time until suffering arises; then people suddenly take their difficulties very much in earnest. As always, the Buddha has the answer: Everything outer and inner is like a dream. It arises, changes and dissolves again. There is a great difference between good and bad experiences. Pleasant experiences created by positive causes liberate us and eventually bring us to enlightenment, while bad ones make us ever more neurotic and weak.

The supreme path of the two Accumulations we just touched upon. It starts with the accumulation of what is positive. This means doing, thinking and saying useful things. In this way, the mind naturally lets go of a few neuroses. Functions which were previously insecure, knotted up, or troubled are now cleared, and we have flashes of insight leading to lasting growth. Thus, out of good actions, arises the understanding that other people are like us; that they also want happiness, try to avoid suffering and behave according to their states of mind. This insight produces more motivation to help them and in this way, step by step, one climbs the ladder to enlightenment. The whole process is so natural that it doesn't need to be proved or disproved, and the fruit is what I call the "non-gluey" Nirvana.

Our mind tends to stick. Either it attaches itself to worldly existence, to appearance and consumption, grasping at that which cannot stay, or it goes to the other extreme and tries not to live, to keep its cool, to not be disturbed, becoming dependent on a state of mere peace. Both are dualistic, and neither corresponds to a full development. Neither confusion nor simple quiet can be a goal. What, then, is the mind's true potential? The "non-gluey" state—recognizing its space-essence in its awareness, its clarity-nature in what happens, and its unlimited quality in the fact that both can be there together, staying spontaneously and effortlessly like that, there is no way that its enlightened potential will not unfold.

THE NEXT VERSE COMES UNDER THE HEADING OF GOAL, WAY AND
PURIFICATION.

The basis of purification is the mind itself in its
    union of clarity and emptiness.
The method of purification is the great
    Mahamudra Diamond-practice.
What is to be purified are the transitory illusory
    impurities.
The fruit of the purification is the perfectly pure
    truth-state. May this become realized.

UNTIL RELIGIOUS COMPETITION FORCED THE LEADING FAITH in the
West to become psychological and to sweeten its coffers,
much precious time was spent on sin and evil. If we really
examine such disturbing factors, however, they are found to
have no powers. Clearly they are only states of mind.

How sinful or dirty can something be that arises from
the purity of free space, plays around there, is understood
through its clarity and returns to its timeless essence again?
The Diamond practice means not believing in their reality
and instead seeing our disturbing feelings as raw material, as
the way in which an untrained mind expresses its power.

The highest level is not to judge, but rather to let thoughts and feelings run their own course while taking care of what is in front of our noses. While handling this wisely and for the good of all, we may occasionally watch the games going on in the zoo of our mind at that particular moment, wondering how we could have taken them seriously. Identifying with the space which is aware, we shall see the tiger getting gradually thinner, the crocodile losing its teeth. Recognizing all impurities to be transitory and illusory, even now, will directly and immensely speed up the process.

Problems only have the power that we give them. If we don't care, how can they disturb us? In all experience we should be aware of the experience, knowing that on the absolute level all things are its free play and thus ultimately pure. When this insight directs the work of lessening negativity, we reach the pure state of enlightenment. Getting out of the troubles caused by confused words, thoughts and actions, the joy and love of space and information being one, arise naturally. Space now contains and doesn't separate us, and from this feeling of joviality and belonging arises every inspiration and insight.

THIS VERSE AGAIN EXPLAINS A "THREESOME" AMONG THE CONDI-
TIONS BRINGING ENLIGHTENMENT.

Overcoming doubts concerning the fundamental
     teaching gives trust in the view.
Protecting this view without distraction is the
     essence of meditation.
Correct meditation in itself is best behavior.
May we trust the view, the meditation and the
     conduct.

ASKING QUESTIONS AND CHECKING THE BUDDHA'S TEACHINGS
will not bring about any need for faith or belief. Everything is totally clear and logical, and if we have doubts, it
usually means that we haven't studied enough. The other
possible cause is that we have mixed up the facts, especially
about what is relative and absolute. The only Buddhist para-
dox I know is whether "countless beings" means a finite or
infinite number, and the next Karmapa will surely be kind
enough to solve that.

Protecting the view means resting in the essence of mind,
trusting it to be naturally perfect. On the relative level, while
still holding changing experiences to be real, it is wise to seed

both mind and surroundings with positive impressions and avoid negative ones. This should always be done from the absolute view, however, knowing that ultimately the timeless radiance of mind surpasses all conditioned experience. Finally, meditation is like cutting a jewel or cleaning a mirror. Every moment in which one remains in clear awareness, eons of confused impressions fall away and the clear light of the mind increases. This, in its very essence, is fearlessness, joy and active compassion, so the more one meditates, the better one will be. The strongest meditation is identifying with and behaving like the Karmapa. His Eminence Situ Rinpoche says that whoever finds from twenty minutes and upwards daily for absorption will not fall down.

Here, some philosophy that makes sense:

All phenomena are projections of the mind.
Mind is not "a" mind; the mind is empty
    in essence.
Although empty, everything constantly arises in it.
Through the deepest examination of the mind
    may we find its innermost root.

In theory, and in non-neurotic states, most people in the West today will admit that experience is subjective, that their feelings color how they see the world. This, however, is only half of what the Karmapa wants to convey. He also wants us to know that what is generally experienced as "outer reality" is of the same nature—also a projection of the mind, that it has no more existence than a collective dream. Clearly, realizing that would mean the end of all hang-ups and immense freedom. How can we go about it?

In countless universes everywhere arise Buddhas, beings who are aware of past, present and future. Out of their love, they manifest whenever conditions permit. Their goal is to free all beings from ignorance and suffering and at first many directly realize their teachings. Then follows a phase when the main emphasis is on meditation. After that people study the teachings and then they can only understand the outer trappings. Later, after a period of further decline, cause and effect are generally forgotten. People become barbaric toward others and themselves and only after much suffering do they become willing to give up so much ego-space that another Buddha can appear. Again the same process is repeated and many are enlightened or liberated before again the wisdom is lost, and another dark period sets in.

After one thousand Buddhas, the world burns up much in the way expected by scientists today, and those who haven't yet recognised the nature of their minds will be attracted by beings of other destroyed universes somewhere in limitless space. When something like a "critical mass" of karma is gathered, gradually another universe arises from the collective tendencies of these beings. Their pride condenses into a solid molecular structure. Collective anger becomes that which is fluid. The attachment of beings appears as heat. Jealousy manifests as constant movement, and stupidity as the experience of space as separation and not as a container. When the complexity of beings has reached a level where they are able to contemplate their own nature, the Buddhas can then manifest and teach. Actually for Asia these five periods which our present Buddha prophesied to be each of five hundred years' length finished thirty to forty years ago. At that time, most traditional Buddhist cultures were either lost to materialism, as in Japan, or to communism in the northern and nationalism in the southern Buddhist world. Today, only Bhutan and the Tibetan refugees can be said to keep alive the whole breadth of the Buddha's teachings there, but luckily many good people are now creating the space for the teaching to live and grow in the West.

That was a long commentary to just one sentence. Here to the rest of the verse:

The mind is not "a" mind, something countable . . . it is empty like space. But who, then, is aware? How can things happen at all? Space, consciousness and the free play of possibilities are all one thing . . . cannot be separated. Through constant awareness of the mind, this is the enlightening insight we seek.

In the following verse, the Karmapa discusses the mind's clarity before its space-nature. Usually today, we explain it in the opposite order.

Self-manifestation, which has never existed as
    such, is erroneously seen as an object.
Through ignorance, self-awareness is mistakenly
    experienced as an "I."
Through attachment to this duality we are caught
    in the conditioned world.
May the root of confusion be found.

WHAT HAPPENS IN THE MIND AND ITS AWARENESS?—neither has any independent existence. Their appearance as such is due to ignorance. What manifests as objects, outer and inner, are really the free play of the mind. Also its clear, limitless space cannot be an "I." There is nothing personal there, and all share the same essence anyway. The former is the mind's richness, the latter its conscious quality. That both can be there shows its unlimited nature. Twenty-five hundred years ago, the Buddha taught: "Form is emptiness, emptiness is form. Form and emptiness cannot be separated." Some years ago during tests in Germany, the smallest particles of the atom simply disappeared. Some years later in America, particles were seen to appear in an absolute vacuum and come into being without apparent physical cause. The more we look at the natural things, the less it is possible to hold a dualistic view. Whatever is and isn't is the same essence manifesting in different ways.

This may sound very academic, but goes far beyond that. The power of both/and consciousness is such that nothing else can even come close. H.H. the 16th Karmapa was one continuous expression of this, transforming all energy into highest bliss. You can find dozens of examples of this in my books. He is the ultimate example that enlightenment is not something intellectual. It is beyond all description, intense and strong.

It is not existent—for even the Buddhas do not
see it.
It is not non-existent, being the basis for both
samsara and nirvana.
It is not the opposites, nor both, nor something
else, but rather their union—the middle way.
May we realize the true nature of mind, which is
beyond extremes.

HERE AGAIN, A FEW LINES SAY EVERYTHING. What reads like
poetry is enlightened philosophy on the highest level,
pointing directly to the nature of mind. Understanding them
is enlightenment, and not being confused about their conditioned existence. On the one side, the mind is not a thing. It
is "empty of" weight, color, smell or size. Thus it cannot be
destroyed, and we should be fearless. On the other side,
however, all things appear in it. Its space is radiant, endowed
with all powers. Knowing this from the level of fearlessness
becomes highest, unceasing joy. Finally seeing it to be inclu-
sive, unlimited and not some subtle substance, it is clear
space, and the search for happiness is seen to be the same in
all, producing strong and active compassion. Is there anything
better one can ask for? Staying in the natural state, everything
perfect arises by itself.

IN THIS VERSE ONCE MORE, THE KARMAPA POINTS TO THE ESSENCE
OF THE MIND.

It cannot be described by saying, "It is."
It cannot be denied by saying, "It is not."
The incomprehensible absolute reality is not
    composite.
May we achieve certainty about the correctness of
    this ultimate meaning.

THE MIND IS NOT A THING, but it manifests all things. The closer we come to the ultimate insight, the less precise are words. They can only express concepts while the experience of mind is all-knowingness and timeless ecstasy. The certainty that this is so is what sets us on the way and makes everything possible.

AND AGAIN:

As long as this is not recognized, the wheel of
    existence turns.
When this is understood, the state of Buddha is
    nothing other than that.
There is nothing that can be described as either
    existing or not existing.
May the nature of reality, the true nature of the
    Buddha mind, be recognized.

AS LONG AS WE DON'T RECOGNIZE THE NATURE OF MIND, our experience will be linear and limited by place and time. One conditioned existence will follow the other, at the same time impressing our mind with the seeds of the situations which will be experienced there. Every painful birth is followed by old age, sickness and death, and while we are here, time is spent fighting for what we want, trying to avoid what we don't want, trying to survive with things we can't avoid, and holding on to what we ultimately cannot keep.

Letting go of fixed concepts and duality, however, all the perfect qualities of mind will unfold and Buddhahood is nothing other than that.

Having already seen that the nature of truth is beyond existence and non-existence, all we need is to rest in awareness itself.

His Eminence Shamar Rinpoche

Appearance is only mind, emptiness is only mind,
    enlightenment is only mind and confusion is
    only one's own mind.
Arising is only mind, disappearance is only mind.
May every doubt and hesitation that concerns the
    mind be overcome.

APPEARANCE IS WHEN MIND EXPRESSES ITS CLARITY AND RICHNESS. Emptiness is the space-nature of mind, its potential. Enlightenment is the recognition of its emptiness, clarity and limitlessness, while confusion means seeing only projections and concepts.

Arising is the mind's free play, and disappearance the return of phenomena to space. How to remove the doubt and hesitation which keeps us from experiencing this? The Buddha advises attack on the outer, inner and secret fronts. Avoiding what is harmful, developing a rich inner life of compassion and wisdom, and identifying with enlightenment—all belong there. On this basis, statements like "first thought, best thought" become reasonable.

My own present understanding of the highest art of living is being conscious on several levels, taking things in parallel while holding the moment in its freshness. One in no way stops the continuity and freshness of direct experience, while at the same time being very aware of the space for conscious change and of how to employ cause and effect. Enjoying the amazing richness of life and at the same time having a ready toolbox for fixing what is less enjoyable on the relative level, I think we are doing very well.

Nothing goes beyond the vibrant energy of direct experience; that is what makes love and excitement so wonderful. Here we forget separation, concepts, past and future, and experience the naked power of mind.

May we neither be sullied by forced intellectual
    meditation nor disturbed by the winds of
    everyday life.
May we skillfully hold onto our practice
    concerning the nature of mind.

HERE WE HAVE THE SECOND NEGATIVE TERM IN THE TEXT, and again it is something to do with impurity. The first time the word denoted duality, the separation of the seer, the thing seen and the process of seeing into a subject, an object and an action. This breaks up the jovial, spontaneous and effortless experience of totality and causes all suffering and limitation.

What merits this second use of the term? What is intellectual and strained meditation? Actually it isn't meditation at all; it is thinking. In Christianity this is similar to "contemplation," pondering deeply over a subject, which is also used by teachers of the Great Way. In the moment, however, when thoughts are made real, meditation is already gone.

In true absorption we rest in the original state, beyond concepts, knowing awareness to be our space and objects our clarity, that both together are our unlimitedness. Then mind

shines naturally like a diamond or an electric bulb, spontaneous and effortless. To sum it up: thoughts are a good slave but
a very bad master, and here we make the strong wish to remain
in our timeless essence and not be distracted or caught by the
conditioned world.

His Eminence Tai Situ Rinpoche

AGAIN, THE KARMAPA CHOOSES NATURAL IMAGERY TO EXEMPLIFY THE WORKINGS OF MIND.

May the immovable ocean of meditative peace,
Where the waves of subtle and gross thoughts
    come to rest through their power, and
Where the waters of the unmoving mind remain
    in themselves,
Unspotted by laziness, sleepiness or unclarity,
    become stable.

THE PICTURES ARE FROM THE BEACH. As the mind comes to rest naturally in its essence, both waves and undertow stop. The resultant clarity manifests as deep, intuitive insight, showing both the ultimate and relative nature of things. We see both its empty nature and also the relative world of appearance.

When thoroughly examined, the radiance of awareness is found to be more fantastic than even the most fascinating pictures it may reflect. The true essence of mind is richer and more meaningful than anything conditioned awareness can bring forth. Our moments of real joy, where things are simply right and the hairs stand up on our arms with joy, are not caused by chasing happiness and seeking to fill our mind with pleasant impressions. They appear when we forget to expect or fear, to spend our energy on past or future, and just relax. Then mind recognizes its timeless nature. This state, when nothing is added to original awareness, is reliable.

Fearlessness, spontaneous joy and active compassion are inseparable from that timeless essence. Whatever is brought about by outer or inner conditions, however, is relative, and there is no way it can stay. Though never prudish and also wishing us every temporal happiness, still the Karmapa advises us to look first for the joy we can rely upon . . . unhindered by laziness, sleepiness and unclarity, mind will discover that it is not neutral. It will understand that it is no white wall where nothing happens if nothing is projected on it. Instead it is rich and fresh . . . highest joy and highest intensity.

THE NEXT VERSE IS A SERIES OF PUNS.

If again and again we examine the mind, which
    cannot be examined,
We see that which cannot be seen, with total
    clarity, just as it is.
May the faultless mind, freed from all doubts
    about being and not being, recognize itself.

THE MIND CANNOT BE EXAMINED BECAUSE IT IS NOT A THING. There is nothing to find. It is empty and unlimited, nor can it see itself from somewhere else. The seer and the thing seen are the same. If it stops looking, however, intuitive insight naturally arises. This conscious quality, its ability to be aware, is its light. There is no outer source. The final wish is that the mind may free itself from all doubts and recognize its faultlessness.

Through the examination of external objects we
  see the mind, not the objects.
Through the examination of the mind we see its
  empty essence, but not the mind.
Through the examination of both, attachment to
  duality disappears by itself.
May the clear light, the true essence of mind, be
  recognized.

ALL EXTERNAL AND INTERNAL PHENOMENA are projections of
mind. If we look at mind, however, we find only space.
Recognizing the empty essence of being and non-being, of me
and you as separate, dualistic concepts simply fall away. This
allows mind's wisdom, joy and compassionate power to unfold.

The Karmapa has just pulled the mole of habitual mind
out of the ground, put contact lenses on its eyes, tied wings
to its paws and feathers to its tail. Now it has to fly like an
eagle. The clear light we want to recognize is nothing but the
timeless essence of mind itself.

Being without intellectual concepts, it is called the
    Great Sign or Mahamudra.
Being without extremes, it is called the Great
    Middle Way, or Madhyamika.
As it embraces everything, it is called the Great
    Perfection, or Maha-Ati.
May we have the confidence that the experience of
    one is the experience of the meaning of all.

AMONG THE TIBETAN WAYS OF INSIGHT, only the Lamdre of the Sakyapas isn't mentioned here. For an "insider" it is fascinating to recognize the "flavor" of the other three schools in the Karmapa's words of 700 years ago. How these energies have attracted teachers and students of a similar bent for so long. We Kagyus are mainly motivated by what we want. Desire and the devotion emphasized in the transmission produce strong experiences and also the tendency to become addicted to them. Our weakness is always waiting for the next blessing and losing energy when they don't appear often enough.

The Mahamudra is appropriate for such people. It brings about a total experience, just like swimming in the ocean. Unlimited by structure and narrowness, it makes us feel warm and at home.

It is also possible to take a sample of water and thus investigate the properties of the ocean. This process is called the great middle way—the Madhyamika—and comes from the intellectual teachings of Sutra and not from the total transmission of experience which is Buddhist Tantra. All Tibetan Buddhists use its positive or neutral understanding of emptiness to explain the nature of reality. In the Gelugpa School, discussions of its philosophical aspects are also the main way to enlightenment, benefitting people who like to take their time and practice gradually.

The third way, Maha-Ati, is also Buddhist Tantra. It is the understanding that all phenomena ultimately self-liberate back into space, and that the truth encompasses everything. This great view attracts people with a tendency towards pride, often ones motivated by what they don't like.

All three views bring ultimate enlightenment and are perfect paths for beings of different aptitudes. To avoid all discussions of "better" or "worse," the Karmapa tells us that whichever way we go, the resultant enlightenment is the same. Thus everybody gets help. Whether we enter through attachment, confusion or anger—the Buddha has thought of us all. Whether we swim in the sea, study a water-sample or observe its surface from a plane: in each case we learn something about H_2O.

His Eminence Jamgon Kongtrul Rinpoche

May we constantly and effortlessly experience the
   never-ending highest joy, which is without
   attachment,
The clear light that is without categories or veils
   of obscuration, and
The spontaneous, concept-free state that is beyond
   intellect.

THE FIRST PHRASE POINTS TO THE CLARITY-NATURE OF MIND. The way fearlessness arises when one recognizes its essence to be indestructible space, highest joy arises through its clarity and power. As this is understood to be timelessly available and richer than anything conditioned that it may manifest, what is there to be attached about? When the sun is out, we don't look much at the moon and stars. Why is the clear light without categories or veils? Its experience is so intense that it simply burns all concepts. This leads to a state of clear insight. Suddenly, life is a gift.

In this verse, the Karmapa takes up some absolute points one last time.

Attachment to pleasant experiences vanishes of its
    own accord.
Illusory and negative thoughts are in their essence
    pure, like space.
In that simple state of mind there is nothing that
    must be given up or developed, avoided or
    attained.
May the truth of the uncomplicated nature of
    reality be realized.

Because enlightenment is intensest joy, everyday attachments lose their power to fetter us. If things are already perfect, nothing can go beyond that. Why is the essence of disturbing thoughts pure like space? Because they arise in it, develop there, are known by space, and disappear back into it again. They have no existence separate from space. The important thing is not to identify with them, to simply let them lie, left and right. In the simple state of mind, where it rests in itself, all enlightened qualities appear naturally. There is nothing to avoid or attain. We make strong wishes to recognize the effortless, natural state of truth.

Here ends the high-altitude flight over the possibilities of mind.

His Eminence Gyaltsap Rinpoche

NEXT, WE PREPARE OURSELVES FOR PASSING ON OUR INSIGHTS TO
OTHERS.

Although the true nature of beings is always the
      Buddha essence,
Still we always wander in the ceaseless wheel of
      life, not understanding that.
May infinite compassion arise for the limitless
      suffering of all beings.

LIMITLESS SUFFERING? Those of us doing well find the state-
ment a bit dramatic. It is a point where Asian and Western
sensitivities differ greatly. However it is only a question of the
level from which life is seen. Compared to full enlightenment,
even our intensest moments are tame, and the contrast is
much greater for ordinary or even unpleasant states.

   The Karmapa's words don't make us poor or small, but
point to an infinite richness. We are all Buddhas, but not
knowing this, we get caught by thoughts and feelings and
miss our timeless clear light.

Although this infinite compassion is strong and
    unceasing,
The truth of its empty nature arises nakedly the
    very moment it appears.
This union of emptiness and compassion is the
    highest faultless way.
May we meditate inseparable from it, the whole
    time, day and night.

COMPASSION IS ACTION, NOT JUST FEELING, and above all there is nothing sugary about it. The moment it arises, we know that it is, in its true nature, empty. Holding compassion and wisdom together, we have both the motivation and a way. We wish to stay in that state always.

May we attain the state of Buddha through
    maturity, realization, and completion,
And develop beings through "divine eyes" and
    "clear sight" arising through the power of
    meditation.
May we realize the Buddha fields and fulfill the
    wishing prayer of the perfection of the
    Buddha qualities.

WHAT DOES "DIVINE EYES" MEAN HERE? If one still has some illusions of an "I" left, it is said that one can "only" see up to 40,000 lifetimes into the past and future. That is an absolute limit for non-Buddhists. Full clarity appears when the emptiness of all things inner and outer has been realized. Then past, present and future are simultaneously there.

The pure Buddha realms are the power-fields appearing from the thirty-seven perfect qualities which Bodhisattvas accumulate along the way. They are safeguards on our path, mental realms from which there is no falling down anymore.

You Buddhas and Bodhisattva from the ten direc-
   tions,
Through your compassion and through the power
   of all the pure and good that exists,
May the pure wishing prayers of ourselves and all
   beings be fulfilled,
Just as they were made.

YOU HAVE RECEIVED HERE A TRANSMISSION OF REAL EXPERIENCE.
From now on a virus is eating its way through the neurosis-programs in your mind. When sometime, in some lifetime, you become rainbows, the decisive factor may have been this prayer.

Nourish the seeds of insight; keep the Mahamudra level as well as you can; nothing is more meaningful. Until you become Buddhas yourselves, at least behave as such.

Afterword

Dear friends,

The last pages of this book became a test of having understood the first. I wrote them on February 5, 1991 under the guns of guerrillas near Bucamaranga in Colombia.

While the commandante took hours declaring the People's war against the gringos—white people—the Colombians from our hijacked bus looked on in pain. All were certain that we would be killed or taken hostage.

It was quite an experience to comment precisely on the nature of mind in that atmosphere . . . its timeless nature had a very special actuality there.

Yours,

Ole
July, 1991

List of Tibetan Buddhist Centers

THE FOLLOWING IS ONLY A PARTIAL LISTING of International Tibetan Buddhist centers authorized by H. H. the Gyalwa Karmapa (Karma Thegsum Choling), and others. We visit as many as possible every year—they are close friends, and you are invited to take part in their programs. For information in North America, contact the Woodstock, New York, center for a comprehensive, updated list; or, in the different countries, call or write directly to the representative centers. Wherever you are, you may always send us a few words at our Copenhagen address. You are welcome everywhere.

UNITED STATES

Karma Triyana
Dharma Chakra
352 Mead Mt. Rd.
Woodstock, NY 12498
(914) 679-2487
Seat in N. America of H. H. Karmapa

Karma Dechen Oser Ling
P.O. Box 2426
San Anselmo, CA 94960
Laurel Bellon: (415) 653-9295
Roland Peters: (415) 821-1815
Ole Nydahl's address in USA

Arizona

KTC c/o Erma Pounds
1338 W. 16th St.
Tempe, AZ 85281
(602) 892-1479

California

Los Angeles KTC
c/o Izabelle Gros
3586 Tacoma Ave.
Los Angeles, CA 90065

Palo Alto KTC
P.O. Box 60793
Palo Alto, CA 94306
(415) 323-7944

Santa Cruz KTC
P.O. Box 8059
Santa Cruz, CA 95061
Lama Dudjom Dorje
(408) 476-0651 / 462-3955

San Diego KTC
904 Edwina Way
Cardiff, CA 92007
(619) 942-2963

Colorado

Marianne Marstrand
P.O. Box 339
Crestone, CO 81131
(719) 256-4698 / 256-4694

New Mexico

Bob & Melani Sachs
214 Girard Blvd. NE
Albuquerque, NM 87106
(505) 265-4826

New York

Lisa Yannios
23-72 36th St.
Astoria, NY 11105
(718) 278-7452

GERMANY

Hamburg KCL
Harkortstieg 4
2000 Hamburg 50
040-3895613

Wuppertal KCL
Heinkelstr. 27
5600 Wuppertal 2
0202-84080

Frankfurt KCL
Wielandstr. 37
6000 Frankfurt
069-5973263

Müchen KCL
Schweppermannstr. 10
8000 München 80
089-493772

Haus Schwarzenberg
Sys Leube
08366-897

AUSTRIA

Wien KCL
Am Fleischmarkt 16
A - 1010 Wien
0043-222-8285434

Graz KCL
St. Peter-Pfarrweg 17
A - 8020 Graz
0043-316-673135

SWITZERLAND

Karma Dorje Ling
Neuarlesheimer Str. 15
CH - 4143 Dornach
0041-61-7018531

Karma Yeshe Gyaltsab Ling
Hammerstr. 9a
CH - 8008 Zurich
0041-1-3820875

DENMARK

Karma Drub Djy Ling
Svanemöllevej 56
DK - 2100 Copenhagen Ö
0045-31-292711

Karma Tcho
Phel Ling Rödby
Korterupvej 21
DK - 4920 Söllested
0045-53-916097

FRANCE

Dhagpo Kagyu Ling
Landrevie / St. Léon s/V
F - 24290 Montignac
0033-53507075

GREECE

Karma Drub Dji Chökhor Ling
Sonierou 15 b, Platia Vathis
GR - 10438 Athens
0030-1-5220218

ITALY

Karme Chö Ling Brescia
Corso Palestro 35
1-25100 Brascia
0039-30-53782

POLAND

Karme Czioe Ling Drobin
Kuchary 57
PL - 9210 Drobin
Vermittl. Drobin Post 56 A

SPAIN

Karma Gön
Atalaya Alta / Apart. 179
E - 9700 Velez-Malaga